MILL FIRE

Sally Nemeth

BROADWAY PLAY PUBLISHING INC
New York
www.broadwayplaypublishing.com
info@broadwayplaypublishing.com

MILL FIRE

© Copyright 2013 by Sally Nemeth

First printing December 2013
I S B N: 978-0-88145-583-0

Book design: Marie Donovan
Page make-up: Adobe Indesign
Typeface: Palatino
Printed and bound in the U S A

ABOUT THE AUTHOR

Sally Nemeth is an award winning playwright and screenwriter. Her plays have been produced by theaters throughout the English-speaking world. Since beginning her television career, she has written for every major network, and produced a documentary film. She is also a published novelist. You can visit her at www.sallynemeth.com.

MILL FIRE received its World Premiere at the Goodman Theatre, Chicago, in April 1989 and was produced in the Studio Theatre. The cast and creative contributors were:

WIDOWS...Martha Lavey
Mary Ann Thebus
Jacqueline Williams
MARLENE..Kelly Coffield
CHAMP...James Krag
SUNNY ....Kate Buddeke
BO .... B J Jones
JEMISON .... Paul Mabon
MINISTER/OSHA INVESTIGATOR..............Timothy Grimm

Director.. David Petrarca
Set design..Linda Buchanan
Costumes ....Laura Cunningham
Lights ....Robert Christen
Sound ....Rob Milburn
Dramaturg .... Tom Creamer
Production stage manager .... David P Foti

In October of 1989, that production moved to New York under the auspices of The Women's Project.

MILL FIRE received its U K premiere in March 1990, produced by the Bush Theatre, London at Riverside Hammersmith Studios. The cast and creative contributors were:

WIDOWS	Barbara Barnes
	Cecilia Noble
	Lynne Verrall
MARLENE	Clare Holman
CHAMP	Steven Hartley
SUNNY	Rosalind March
BO	Stephen Hoye
JEMISON	Bob Wisdom
MINSTER/OSHA INVESTIGATOR	Michael McManus
Director	Brian Stirner
Set design	Michael Taylor
Costumes	Sue Born-Thompson
Lights	Rick Fisher
Music	Mandy More
Sound design	Colin Brown
Dialect coach	Joan Washington
Production stage manager	Kate Beeston

CHARACTERS

MARLENE, *25 years old, high-school education, office worker.*

CHAMP, *late 20s,* MARLENE's *husband. Steelworker.*

SUNNY, *mid-to-late 30s.* MARLENE's *sister-in-law. Does not work.*

BO, *pushing 40, beginning to thicken.* MARLENE's *brother. Steel mill foreman, Vietnam vet.*

JEMISON, *also around 40. A substantial black man. Also a foreman.*

MINISTER, *mid 30s. Alabama Baptist, but not sanctimonious. Doubles as the* OSHA INVESTIGATOR.

WIDOWS 1, 2, & 3, *even though they speak as a sort of collective consciousness and are dressed alike, they should be as distinct physically as possible. They should be of different age, race, height etc. They are not the same woman.*

NOTE

This text is the Goodman Theatre production draft.
The physical limitations of the stage partially dictated
the design. In the Goodman studio, the area dedicated
to the BO/SUNNY scenes was a small kitchen space. In
the U K production, as in the original conception, that
space was a bedroom. The BO/SUNNY scenes take on
a slightly different dynamic when played in a kitchen
rather than in a bedroom, but both work equally well.
The choice is yours.

ACT ONE

(Late 1970s. Birmingham, Alabama. The stage should be divided into various areas, not necessarily by scenery, but often with lights. Distinctions need to be made between the following areas: CHAMP *and* MARLENE's *bed,* BO *and* SUNNY's *kitchen, the mill, the church. It is helpful to have levels on the stage—a catwalk or scaffolding—and staircases leading to the upper level. At the top of the play, the widows sit downstage, veiled in tulle and dressed in black, sipping from white coffee cups. The bed is draped in a sooty tarp. The widows go to the bed and remove the tarp, revealing* MARLENE, *lying on the bed in a slip.)*

MARLENE: In the hottest part of a hot July day, I lie on the bed, a fan oscillating over me, a tall glass of tea on the bedside table. Beads forming on the glass, sweat beads, running down its sides. A ring of water, ruining the finish on the table top. My skin still hot after my second shower of the day. Hot to the touch. My arms and legs arranged so as to leave space between. Breathing space. Space to let my hot skin breathe. You know what I mean? How that is?

CHAMP: *(He appears, standing at the head of the bed in a full steelworkers' heat-reflective suit, hardhat, safety glasses and gloves.)* Yeah.

MARLENE: And hot as I am, with my limbs arranged to avoid contact with one another I want you next to me. In that heat I want you there. I think you there.

And there you are. I start to feel good. The heat doesn't bother me. It all goes away. Everything goes away except you and me and the bed. Sometimes in the afternoon there's a thunderstorm.

CHAMP: Sometimes.

MARLENE: Sometimes there is. The curtains start to blow and my head starts to clear like all the worry in the world will never be mine. And when the hard rain cores pouring over the sills we don't get up and close the windows. We let it pour over the sills, soaking the rug, warping the floorboards. Because none of those things are there. Nothing is there except you and me and the bed.

CHAMP: Nothing's there.

MARLENE: Not a thing. You, me, and the bed.

(CHAMP *disappears.*)

MARLENE: Nothing. No thing, no body.

SUNNY: (*Knocks at door*) Marlene? Marlene honey, wake up.

MARLENE: I'm not asleep.

SUNNY: (*Entering room. She is dressed in dark clothing and carries a black dress and panty hose over her shoulder.*) You're not.

MARLENE: No, I'm not.

SUNNY: Well, you're not now, but you were then.

MARLENE: How do you know.

SUNNY: You were talking up a storm.

MARLENE: So?

SUNNY: I guess you were talking in your sleep.

MARLENE: You guess.

SUNNY: O K. You were talking to yourself and now we all got to worry about you.

MARLENE: Why.

SUNNY: Everybody's going to think you're a crazy lady.

MARLENE: Don't they already.

SUNNY: Maybe you'd like them to. *(Takes dress and stockings off her shoulder and lays them on the bed)*

MARLENE: What is that.

SUNNY: What does it look like? I'm not wearing that.

MARLENE: I threw that in the Goodwill bag.

SUNNY: And I took it out.

MARLENE: It's not touching my skin.

SUNNY: Well, what are you going to wear?

MARLENE: Not that. *(Hurls dress to the floor)*

SUNNY: It's the only dark thing you've got.

MARLENE: Oh, for Christ's sake. I'm not going to do that. I'm not going to make everybody else comfortable because I'm behaving appropriately.

SUNNY: I don't see any point in that. *(Retrieves dress, lays it out)*

MARLENE: You don't.

SUNNY: No, I don't.

MARLENE: That doesn't surprise me. Where's Bo?

SUNNY: Coming from the mill with the rest of the shift.

MARLENE: Showing in numbers.

SUNNY: What did you expect? They're going to stay away?

MARLENE: That wouldn't be appropriate.

SUNNY: Goes a little deeper than that.

MARLENE: Can't tempt fate.

SUNNY: Marlene, you are full of shit, you know that?

MARLENE: I've never known more superstitious men than steelworkers. Have you?

SUNNY: That's shit. How can you even think things like that—especially about your own goddamn brother. And how do you think I feel when you say things like that about Bo.

MARLENE: You tell me.

SUNNY: He's my husband. That's how I feel when you say things like that. I mean, I've let a lot of things slide.

MARLENE: Oh. Well.

SUNNY: Listen, anniversaries are hard. Bringing it all back up again. But lay off Bo. He feels awful. They all do.

MARLENE: They can feel as awful as they want. And the anniversary is no harder than the day to day. Can't bring anything back up again that never went away.

SUNNY: Give it time.

MARLENE: Oh, Sunny, that's some fine advice. I think I'll take it to heart.

SUNNY: Wear what you want. We'll be leaving for the church in a half an hour.

MARLENE: I don't need an escort. Tell Bo.

SUNNY: You tell him. Half hour.

(SUNNY *exits.* MARLENE *dresses in a very colorful dress. The* WIDOWS *enter, unveiled, and will move to an observer's position on the upper level.*)

WIDOW 1: They'd swung over to graveyard shift a day or two before. He never could sleep those first couple days after the shift had changed.

WIDOW 2: Never could sleep. Went to work tired. Came home tired. Then the sun would come out and it didn't matter if the drapes were drawn or the kids were quiet.

WIDOW 3: It was never quiet enough or dark enough.

WIDOW 1: And I'd slip around the house.

WIDOW 3: Getting the kids ready for school. Myself ready for work. And he'd toss.

WIDOW 2: Rolling back and forth on the bed. The sound of the mill still in his ears.

WIDOW 1: And the kids would be ready and I'd be ready and I'd unplug the phone and lock the door behind me.

WIDOW 2: Come home at three with the kids to find him up and having a beer.

WIDOW 1: Couldn't ever sleep. Too light. Too loud.

WIDOW 3: Even those two days before. When it rained and rained.

WIDOW 2: That sound of rain. That lulling sound. On the roof. Dripping from the gutters.

WIDOW 1: Even that didn't do it. I'd come home that day to find him up.

WIDOW 2: Having a beer and a sandwich.

WIDOW 3: I said I'd fix him something hot to eat but he said he didn't want it.

WIDOW 1: It didn't feel like it was time to eat something hot. It wasn't just the sleep. It was food too.

WIDOW 3: He said he never knew when he was coming or going. Never knew.

(SUNNY *enters the kitchen with a bag of groceries. She takes a pint bottle of whiskey from the bag and puts it in her purse. She replaces the receiver of the wall phone back on the cmddle, and starts to put things away, calling up the stairs to* Bo. *It is night, and it is raining.)*

SUNNY: Bo, Bo honey, wake up.

Bo: Yeah.

SUNNY: It's time to get up.

Bo: What time is it?

(Bo *comes down the stairs in his underwear and takes a seat at the table.* SUNNY *sets a place before him.)*

SUNNY: Nine.

Bo: First time I've slept straight through in the past couple days.

SUNNY: It's the rain. Makes it cooler. Darker.

Bo: I guess.

SUNNY: Jemison called from the mill, but I told him I wasn't going to wake you until nine.

Bo: Sunny—you know to wake me.

SUNNY: First time you've slept in days.

Bo: What did he want?

SUNNY: Creek's up.

Bo: Into the mill?

SUNNY: Part of it. He said one furnace is out.

Bo: Shit.

SUNNY: He just wants you to call him.

Bo: *(He heads up the stairs.)* You should have just woken me up.

SUNNY: Yeah, we've been through that. What do you want to eat?

Bo: I don't know. What did you have?

SUNNY: Tuna casserole.

BO: No. Why don't you just fix me some eggs.

SUNNY: How do you want them.

BO: Surprise me.

(CHAMP *is in bed asleep.* MARLENE *enters.*)

MARLENE: Champ, baby it's nine o'clock.

CHAMP: So?

MARLENE: So get up. Your shift rolled over two days ago.

CHAMP: I know.

MARLENE: And you left me a note to come get you at nine.

CHAMP: Well come on girl. Come and get me.

MARLENE: What time you got to be there?

CHAMP: Eleven thirty or so. We won't do shit out there with this rain. Just sit around and collect pay.

MARLENE: Best kind of work to have.

CHAMP: Come here.

MARLENE: I'm here.

(MARLENE *gets into bed and curls up against* CHAMP. *Shift over to kitchen, where the phone is ringing.* BO *runs down the stairs to get it, more or less dressed in mill clothes. He will button, tie, zip, etc. as he talks.*)

BO: Yeah, I got your message. (*Pause, laughs*) Well, she knows what happens when she don't let me sleep. So, what have we got. Uh huh. Well I can't do much with that. I know that. Yeah. I know. (*Pause*) Well my shift ain't the only one's not up to quota... Yeah I know you know. (*Pause*) How many heats? With one furnace out. That's ridiculous. I mean I guess we can do it we keep the other two fired all night.

BO: *(Pause)* When have I had a choice? All right man. I'll be down right away. Bye. *(Hangs up. begins to tie shoes, remembers* CHAMP, *and redials phone.)* Champ, you awake? Well why didn't you let Marlene answer.

*(*SUNNY *enters in a robe with a cup of coffee.)*

BO: Oh. Well, any way I won't be able to give you a ride in tonight. I got to go early. Unless you want to go when I do. *(Pause)* Didn't think so. All right. See you before midnight.

*(*BO *hangs up.* SUNNY *comes in with a cup of coffee.)*

BO: You fix them eggs yet?

SUNNY: I was waiting for you to come down.

*(*SUNNY *hands* BO *coffee.)*

BO: Well don't. I got to be off now.

SUNNY: How long are a couple eggs going to take.

BO: You got to cook them then I got to sit and eat them and I hate to shovel my food.

SUNNY: Then don't. Sit down and eat like a human being. They can wait another half hour.

BO: I said I'd be right down.

SUNNY: I haven't seen you to say boo to in some time.

BO: Well I'm not going to make conversation sitting and shoveling eggs.

SUNNY: Fine. You're just going to shovel doughnuts or some shit when you get to the mill anyway.

BO: Then fix some damn eggs.

SUNNY: Fix them yourself.

*(*SUNNY *heads up the stairs,* BO *grabs his jacket and exits the house. Shift over to* CHAMP *and* MARLENE *in bed.)*

MARLENE: What did he want?

CHAMP: He's going in early. Can't give me a ride.

MARLENE: Something wrong?

CHAMP: I don't know. I guess if he's going in early. You need the car?

MARLENE: Not till morning.

CHAMP: I hate to leave you without a car.

MARLENE: I'm not going anywhere. Except to bed.

CHAMP: You're already there.

MARLENE: Yeah, I know it. Damn Bo.

CHAMP: Why?

MARLENE: I don't know. Since it's raining and all I kind of thought I might could talk you into maybe calling in sick.

CHAMP: Well, I can't do that now I've talked with him.

MARLENE: Maybe we could have car trouble.

CHAMP: That's pushing it.

MARLENE: I guess. But you know how I get when it rains.

CHAMP: I know how you get.

MARLENE: So come on. Car died. What do you think?

CHAMP: Girl, you're crazy.

MARLENE: You love it.

CHAMP: Don't I though.

(CHAMP *exits.*)

MARLENE: Champ! (*Chases after him*)

(*Shift over to* BO *and* JEMISON *in the mill area*)

JEMISON: It's nearest the creek.

BO: Fucking poor planning.

JEMISON: You said it.

BO: So what's the story?

JEMISON: We're way behind.

BO: Like I don't know it. Everyone's been crawling up my butt all week.

JEMISON: Mine too.

BO: So we need to make at least five heats on each furnace of seventy grade. That's it, right?

JEMISON: You got it.

BO: It can be done. If we don't lose another furnace.

JEMISON: Never happen.

BO: Bullshit.

JEMISON: (*Pulls cigarettes out of his front pocket. They are soaked.*) Shit. These are all wet. You got a smoke?

BO: (*Pulls a pack of Lucky Strikes out of his pocket*) Always do.

(BO *and* JEMISON *light up.*)

BO: So what's the big fucking hurry on this seventy grade?

JEMISON: Big highway project up north.

BO: Yeah?

JEMISON: Yeah. Construction company swung over to us after the mill supplying them went on strike. So they cleaned us out of our inventory and want more. Yesterday. You know.

BO: Nice to get a contract like that.

JEMISON: Sure, if we can do it. And you know, front office will say anything. A million tons tomorrow? No problem.

BO: I'm just as glad.

JEMISON: Yeah.

Bo: The way things are going and all. It's good to have orders coming in.

JEMISON: So long as we deliver. I mean, we fuck up on this, and another might not come our way.

Bo: Don't I know it.

JEMISON: Did you hear about U S?

Bo: What—they striking again?

JEMISON: Hell no. They got no leverage at all. Here's what I heard. They're closing down their rolling mill.

Bo: No.

JEMISON: Yeah. Just keeping the melt shop open, then taking the steel elsewhere to mill it.

Bo: Jesus.

JEMISON: They'll be laying off a couple thousand men.

Bo: Shit. Where'd you hear that?

JEMISON: It's been flying around for a while.

Bo: How come I didn't hear that?

JEMISON: I don't know.

Bo: Well, I've got some time to kill here. Is there any coffee on?

JEMISON: Been on for a while. You might want to make some fresh.

Bo: I'll do that.

JEMISON: There's some doughnuts in there too. Help yourself.

(Bo *and* JEMISON *exit. The* WIDOWS *enter with* MARLENE, *and sit in chairs with their coffee cups.* MARLENE *lights a cigarette.*)

WIDOW 1: It cleared that morning. Cleared and the sun came out hot and bright.

WIDOW 2: Everything got steamy. All that wet ground. Oversoaked and steaming.

WIDOW 3: I wanted the rain back again. Wanted the dark, the gloom of it. It seemed that was more in keeping with everything else.

WIDOW 2: Wanted that sound. To hear water rolling off the roof.

WIDOW 1: The cicadas came out to dry their wings. Thousands of them. Millions. Setting up that buzz.

WIDOW 3: The buzz came in waves, like they planned when they were going to get loud. When they were going to get softer.

WIDOW 2: And I listened to that. The cicadas. Let it wash over me. Let it roll off the roof.

WIDOW 1: The bugs buzzing and the house full of people, relatives, friends, buzzing.

(The MINISTER *enters and pours a cup of coffee.*)

WIDOW 3: The kids crying. Not really sure what was going on, but crying because everyone else was.

MARLENE: Except me. I was listening to the buzz. Going right through me.

MINISTER: Mrs Hotchkiss? Mrs Hotchkiss—would you like some coffee?

MARLENE: Coffee?

MINISTER: Would you like some?

MARLENE: No. No coffee. Thank you.

MINISTER: Well, if you're sure.

(No response)

MINISTER: Well, it's good to see you again, though of course I wish the circumstances were different.

MARLENE: You said that last year.

WIDOW 1: Marlene.

MARLENE: What.

WIDOW 1: Don't start. Please. Not tonight.

MARLENE: I don't see what's so damn different about tonight. Three hundred sixty five days. Each one of them the same.

WIDOW 2: I hear you.

MINISTER: Marlene—may I call you Marlene?

MARLENE: Everyone else does.

MINISTER: I believe that—I believe that what we're here to do tonight is a healing thing. It was a senseless accident that took your husbands. Folks need to work it out. They need to bring it up again so it doesn't stay way down deep inside them.

MARLENE: Oh, I don't think this has gone too far below the surface.

WIDOW 1: Marlene, why are you here?

WIDOW 3: Can't we just be—

WIDOW 1: No, I can't. Marlene here has yanked us around but good.

WIDOW 2: I don't think she did what she did to yank anybody around.

WIDOW 1: You were talking something different back when the mill was ready to yank the settlement.

WIDOW 2: Well I've had some time now to think about it.

WIDOW 1: So have I. So why are you here Marlene?

MARLENE: I'm here to heal. How about you?

(They exit. Shift over to SUNNY, who comes to the kitchen table and pours herself a drink from her bottle. She has had a

few. She opens a magazine and leafs through it briskly, then notices the placesetting BO *left behind.)*

SUNNY: Fuck you Bo, fuck you Bo, fuck you.

(SUNNY *clears the placesetting, then goes back to her magazine. The phone rings three or four times before she answers.)*

SUNNY: What. No Marlene, he's already gone. Uh. huh. Well, I'm sorry to hear that but I'm going to be using my car tonight. Yeah. Well, sounds like all you need is a jump. Right. Well, he's got to be there by now—left here like a house afire. Have Champ call him there. Bye. (*Hangs up. Freshens her drink.)* I'm going out tonight. Sure. Gonna have me a good time.

(SUNNY *takes phone off the hook and goes upstairs. Shift over to* CHAMP *and* MARLENE's *bedroom. They enter.)*

CHAMP: Why did you ask her for the car?

MARLENE: I knew she'd say no.

CHAMP: How'd you know that.

MARLENE: I just knew.

CHAMP: Is she drunk?

MARLENE: (*Gets into bed)* Champ.

CHAMP: Is she?

MARLENE: On her way there.

CHAMP: Well, that pretty much settles it.

MARLENE: What.

CHAMP: (*Gets into bed with her)* I got to go in tonight.

MARLENE: Aw, Champ.

CHAMP: Bo's a son of a bitch when Sunny's hitting it.

MARLENE: He can be.

CHAMP: He is. You've seen it.

MARLENE: Yeah.

CHAMP: Sometimes I don't see it—the two of them.

MARLENE: You don't.

CHAMP: Not at all.

MARLENE: He loves the fucking steel mill and all she does is drive him there.

CHAMP: What does she get out of it?

MARLENE: What do you think she gets out of it?

CHAMP: I'm asking you.

MARLENE: She gets to be "poor Sunny".

CHAMP: Poor Sunny.

MARLENE: Poor Sunny. No kids and that man who don't pay her no attention.

CHAMP: Bo's lacking in some of the finer points.

MARLENE: That ain't all he's lacking.

CHAMP: That's not fair.

MARLENE: Fair or not, you know that's what it is and what it's about.

CHAMP: Wasn't nothing she didn't know about.

MARLENE: They were married before he went.

CHAMP: So?

MARLENE: So, you don't divorce no fucking purple heart. Not in Sunny's book.

CHAMP: What time's it getting to be?

MARLENE: Around ten.

CHAMP: You want to fix me something to eat?

MARLENE: *(Getting amorous)* No I don't want to fix you something to eat.

CHAMP: You don't.

MARLENE: No.

CHAMP: Why not?

MARLENE: Because I want you to eat me.

CHAMP: Fix me something to eat first.

MARLENE: I don't want to.

CHAMP: I'll faint. Pass out cold. Everything's starting to go—dark. *(He slumps over, not to be roused.)*

MARLENE: Champ. Champ, come on. Champ. Shit. *(Gets out of bed)* How do you want your eggs?

(CHAMP grabs at MARLENE's feet as she exits.)

(Shift over to BO, munching on a doughnut with a styrofoam cup of coffee in his hand in the mill area. JEMISON holds a clipboard.)

BO: What kind of scrap we got?

JEMISON: Automotive.

BO: Shit.

JEMISON: Yeah, it's pretty wet.

BO: Holds water like a sponge.

JEMISON: Some of it's under cover, but you'll go through it pretty quick.

BO: We'll just use the wet stuff for the first melt and charge the heats with the drier stuff.

JEMISON: Yeah. I been doing that.

BO: Ain't you smart.

JEMISON: Not too. I started off throwing anything in before I knew how wet it was.

BO: Kaboom.

JEMISON: Yeah. You know. The furnace is capped off. You know it, and the guys know it but it still scares the shit out of them.

BO: Oh yeah.

JEMISON: A couple guys dove for cover.

BO: Who?

JEMISON: Pritchett and Turn.

BO: Yeah?

JEMISON: And you know with all the other noise I'm surprised anyone hears it. It don't make that big a bang.

BO: It's big enough.

JEMISON: You're still going to run out of dry scrap. Maybe mid-shift.

BO: I run out, I'll figure it out. You know.

JEMISON: *(Hands over clipboard)* I know.

MARLENE: *(Entering with the* MINISTER*)* What.

MINISTER: Marlene.

MARLENE: What.

MINISTER: Look. This isn't easy for any of them either.

MARLENE: You don't think I know that?

MINISTER: I wasn't sure.

MARLENE: I do. Real well. Real well.

MINISTER: May I ask you something?

MARLENE: You can ask.

MINISTER: How old are you?

MARLENE: Shit. I thought it was going to be something important.

MINISTER: Important?

MARLENE: Yeah. So solemn. "May I ask you something?

MINISTER: Well?

MARLENE: Twenty-five. Now you going to tell me I got my whole life ahead of me?

MINISTER: No.

MARLENE: No?

MINISTER: Not exactly.

MARLENE: But something along those lines.

MINISTER: You're just— You're awfully hard for a woman of twenty-five.

MARLENE: You got any better ideas?

MINISTER: I don't understand.

MARLENE: On how to behave. You got any ideas for me. Do you? Because I'm open to ideas. But I don't know a whole lot of twenty-five year old widows and I don't know a whole lot of other ways to get myself to tomorrow and the next day and the next day— *(Begins to break a little bit)*

MINISTER: Marlene— *(Reaches to her and places his hand on her shoulder)* I didn't mean to upset you.

MARLENE: Yes you did.

MINISTER: Yes I did.

MARLENE: Hold me.

MINISTER: Marlene, I—

MARLENE: Please, just do it.

(MINISTER *holds* MARLENE. *Very stiffly. He is totally uncomfortable. She holds him and tries to get relaxed into him. He still doesn't relax. She pulls away.)*

MINISTER: I'm sorry. I've never—I've been asked for all kinds of solace, but I've never had a parishoner ask to be physically comforted.

MARLENE: I'm not a parishoner. I'm a twenty-five year old widow. *(Pause)* I haven't been held in a year.

MINISTER: Marlene, I'm sorry. I—you're a twenty-five year old widow.

MARLENE: With a hard edge.

MINISTER: No.

MARLENE: Are you a Methodist?

MINISTER: Baptist.

MARLENE: You hug like you've got a corncob up your butt.

(MARLENE *and* MINISTER *look at one another for a moment, then laugh. They exit. The* WIDOWS *appear above)*

WIDOW 3: Oh yes, the children are quite a comfort to me.

WIDOW 2: Quite a comfort.

WIDOW 1: The youngest still crawls up into my lap when I'm watching the T V at night.

WIDOW 2: Leans into me and falls asleep.

WIDOW 1: I carry him upstairs and put him to bed. Tuck him between cartoon sheets.

WIDOW 3: Brush the hair away from his father's forehead.

WIDOW 1: His father's face.

WIDOW 2: My big boy is getting too old to be held.

WIDOW 3: That's what he says.

(Shift over to CHAMP *in bed, asleep.* MARLENE *enters.)*

MARLENE: Get up.

CHAMP: I'm up.

MARLENE: No you're not.

CHAMP: Well I am now.

MARLENE: You want some eggs or don't you?

CHAMP: I want some.

MARLENE: You got to be awake to eat them.

CHAMP: I'm awake.

MARLENE: You always do this.

CHAMP: Well girl, you wear me out.

MARLENE: No I don't.

CHAMP: Yeah you do.

MARLENE: I do.

CHAMP: Yeah.

MARLENE: Shit.

CHAMP: I'm not complaining.

MARLENE: Good.

CHAMP: What time is it?

MARLENE: Eleven.

CHAMP: *(Gets out of bed)* Were you going to let me oversleep?

MARLENE: I thought about it.

CHAMP: Good choice.

MARLENE: *(Gets into bed)* Says you.

CHAMP: Well I'll be back in eight hours. Then you can call in sick.

MARLENE: Maybe I will.

CHAMP: Maybe.

MARLENE: I got a whole eight hours to sleep on it.

(CHAMP *exits. Shift up to the* WIDOWS, *still above)*

WIDOW 2: This is what I liked. Right were his butt went in. That indentation that men have and women don't. Boy, I like that.

WIDOW 3: His hands were amazing. They were always being banged up at work. His right hand ring finger went every which way. Scars all over from burns and cuts. But the way he moved them. They looked almost pretty.

WIDOW 1: My man was definitely packing it on. Right across the middle. Getting stretch marks on his lower back. All the other men in his family were spindly. He got a kick out of it. He loved his little gut.

(Shift to the mill)

JEMISON: Bo. Hey. Your wife's on the phone.

BO: What does she want?

SUNNY: Didn't ask.

BO: All right.

(BO gets on the mill phone, while SUNNY is on the ktchen phone.)

BO: Yeah.

SUNNY: I want you home now. I want you home.

BO: Sunny—I can't do that. I'm at work.

SUNNY: I don't care.

BO: I'm up to my neck in water and I can't—

SUNNY: Oh, it's always a crisis. Always a fucking crisis.

BO: Sunny, you don't seem to understand.

SUNNY: I understand fine. I just don't care. You hear me? I just don't care.

BO: I hear you.

SUNNY: You hear me.

BO: Sunny, listen, I'll be home in the morning. We can talk then.

SUNNY Yeah we can. But we won't.

BO: I swear to you honey.

SUNNY: Because I won't be here in the morning.

(SUNNY *hangs up and exits. Shift over to* CHAMP *and* MARLENE. *Phone rings.*)

MARLENE: Hello? Hang on, he's just getting ready to head out. (*Covers receiver and hollers*) Champ! Honey! It's Bo! (*Back to phone*) Why you at work so early? Yeah. Uh-huh. That doesn't sound good.

(CHAMP *enters.*)

MARLENE: Here's Champ. Oh, O K. Yeah, I talked to her not too long ago. (*Pause*) Listen, don't worry about it. No, don't. You got enough to worry about tonight. (*Pause*) Hey, Bo, I'm sorry. I know you know. Yeah. Bye. (*Hangs up*)

CHAMP: What was that about?

MARLENE: He wants you to go over to his house and take Sunny's car keys away.

CHAMP: What?

MARLENE: You heard me.

CHAMP: Why?

MARLENE: Said she called him, loaded, and told him she was taking off.

CHAMP: Well, that's something new.

MARLENE: Yeah, it is.

CHAMP: Shit.

MARLENE: I'm sorry, baby, it's just—

CHAMP: No, it's O K.

MARLENE: You know he doesn't like to drag you into this.

CHAMP: I'm family.

MARLENE: Not blood.

MARLENE: I'm still family.

MARLENE: Well, you know Bo.

CHAMP: Yeah, I know Bo. *(Pause)* I better get.

MARLENE: Yeah.

CHAMP: Hey, you want to come with me?

MARLENE: No.

CHAMP: I could just take Sunny's car and you could keep ours.

MARLENE: No.

CHAMP: Come. on.

MARLENE: You know how it goes. I get over there I'll never get out.

CHAMP: It was worth a try.

MARLENE: It's always worth a try.

CHAMP: Yeah. *(Kisses her)* See you in the morning.

MARLENE: Drive careful.

(CHAMP *exits. Shift over to* BO *at the mill. He takes a pill bottle out of his shirt pocket and takes two.* JEMISON *approaches him.)*

JEMISON: Jeff Smyer called while you were on the other line.

BO: To say what.

JEMISON: He ain't comin' in.

BO: What?

JEMISON: He ain't comin' in.

BO: Why not.

JEMISON: His cellar flooded and a wall's caved in.

BO: He ain't going to change that by being there.

JEMISON: No, he ain't.

BO: Shit. If it was me I'd come to work. I wouldn't stand around like no asshole and watch my house go down.

JEMISON: *(Goes to a locker, takes off his mill jacket and changes into a street jacket)* My old place? I'd stand there and cheer it on.

BO: Yeah?

JEMISON: Yeah. I'd love to see it go down. Collect insurance. Build me a brand new house. New wiring, plumbing. I'd love to see that happen.

BO: Them old houses are built.

JEMISON: Yeah.

BO: Make it through a tornado.

JEMISON: Yeah.

BO: There's something to be said for that.

JEMISON: I don't know what. Hey man, I'm out of here.

BO: *(Heading him off)* Listen, can you hang on until Champ gets here?

JEMISON: Aw man, I'm beat.

BO: I know, but Smyer's out and Champ's running late. I just need another body.

JEMISON: *(Returning to locker resignedly and changing back into his mill jacket)* All right, but Champ better hurry his ass.

BO: He's on his way.

(SUNNY enters with a suitcase, which she opens and puts on a kitchen chair. She exits and returns with a pile of laundry.)

CHAMP: *(Enters tentatively)* Sunny?

SUNNY: Oh Jesus.

CHAMP: I'm sorry, did I scare you?

SUNNY: Champ?

CHAMP: Yeah.

SUNNY: What are you doing here?

CHAMP: I'm here to see if you're all right.

SUNNY: *(Sorting out* BO's *laundry and packing her own in the suitcase, sloppily)* If I'm all right.

CHAMP: Yeah. Bo was worried about you. He asked me to look in on you on my way to work.

SUNNY: He did.

CHAMP: Yeah.

SUNNY: Well, isn't that something.

CHAMP: So I'm looking in on you.

SUNNY: Do I look all right?

CHAMP: Fine.

SUNNY: All right then.

CHAMP: Sunny—I need—

SUNNY: What do you need?

CHAMP: I need your keys. To borrow your rear.

SUNNY: Didn't I tell Marlene—

CHAMP: Marlene's waiting out in our car and I need to borrow yours so she can have ours.

SUNNY: Marlene's in the car? Well why don't she come in? *(Heads over to window and hollers out)* Marlene! Hey Marlene. Get the hell in here girl. *(She turns from the window.)* Champ, honey, I hate to tell you this but Marlene ain't in your car.

CHAMP: I know.

SUNNY: And she ain't in the house.

CHAMP: O K. Bo asked me to get your keys.

SUNNY: He did.

CHAMP: Yeah.

SUNNY: Well you can't have them.

CHAMP: Come on Sunny.

SUNNY: No.

CHAMP: You shouldn't be driving.

SUNNY: I shouldn't.

CHAMP: No. The roads are awful.

SUNNY: Oh. You're concerned for my safety. I see. Well that's different.

CHAMP: Where are your keys?

SUNNY: Nowhere.

CHAMP: *(Picks up her purse)* Are they in here?

SUNNY: You stay out of my bag.

CHAMP: Are they in here?

SUNNY: You stay out of that.

(CHAMP *reaches in the bag.)*

SUNNY: Stay out of that.

(SUNNY *launches herself at* CHAMP. *He comes up with the keys. She hits at him.)*

SUNNY: You son of a bitch.

CHAMP: *(He restrains her.)* Sunny.

SUNNY: Son of a bitch.

CHAMP: Sunny. Sunny. Shhh. Shhh. *(He holds her from behind, pinning her arms down to her sides. He rocks her.)* That's right. That's right.

SUNNY: *(Begins to cry)* You know. I've had a bad day. A real bad day.

CHAMP: I know. I know.

SUNNY: No you don't. You don't know.

CHAMP: I know.

SUNNY: You don't. *(Struggles in his hold)*

CHAMP: Sunny! *(Restrains her)*

SUNNY: Oh shit. *(Long pause)* Listen to that. Listen to that rain.

(SUNNY gets sexual in the hold. CHAMP releases her.)

CHAMP: It's coming down hard.

SUNNY: Off and on like that. All day. At that house caticorner there was a kid sitting on the porch playing *Swanee River* over and over on his harmonica. Badly. Over and over. Rain pouring over the eaves like a curtain. And this kid. Probably driving his mama crazy so she sent him outside to drive the rest of us nuts. And there's Bo asleep upstairs. *Swanee River* over and over. Banging into my head. Thinking Bo's gonna wake up. That's going to wake him up. I pull my coat over my head and start across the street to talk to this boy's mama. I don't know these people. They're new on the street. They don't know most folks in the neighborhood work swing shifts. I need to tell them. I need to represent my community. Today I am civic minded. I get over to the porch and I look at this kid. His eyes are way too far apart. His mouth is funny. He smiles. So big. Hollers, "MamaMamaCompanyMama!" And now I don't know what to say. What can I say? Your idiot child is making me crazy?

CHAMP: Sunny, if you're all right now I'll—

SUNNY: I got down on my knees and that child threw his arms around me and I held on. Held on so the ground wouldn't open up underneath me. His mama come to the door and I said to her, "He's a wonderful boy." And she said, "Yes, he is."

CHAMP: Sunny. I'm gonna be late now. You O K?

SUNNY: O K? Yeah, I'm—

CHAMP: *(Pause)* All right then. *(He starts to exit.)*

SUNNY: Hey Champ.

CHAMP: *(He pauses.)* Yeah?

SUNNY: I don't know. I thought I married well. What do you think?

CHAMP: Good night Sunny. *(Exits)*

SUNNY: *(Pauses, then yells)* I asked you a question!

(SUNNY heads upstairs. MARLENE enters, smoking a cigarette. WIDOW 1 approaches her.)

WIDOW 1: You and the Reverend have a nice talk?

MARLENE: We talked.

WIDOW 1: Uh-huh. *(Pause)* You got another cigarette?

MARLENE: Sure. *(Takes a pack from her pocket and hands it over)*

WIDOW 1: *(Takes cigarette out of pack, hands the pack back)* You got a light?

MARLENE: *(Hands over her own cigarette)* You'll have to jump start. I'm out of matches.

WIDOW 1: *(Jumps her cigarette. Hands lit cigarette back to MARLENE.)* I'm smoking a lot these days.

MARLENE: I always smoked a lot.

WIDOW 1: I try not to with the kids. Don't want them smoking.

MARLENE: They probably won't if you do. They got to be different.

WIDOW 1: I suppose that's true. My folks didn't smoke. My daddy chewed some.

MARLENE: I think that's worse.

WIDOW 1: Yeah. With the spitting and all. *(Pause)* Mind if I ask you something.

MARLENE: Everybody's full of questions tonight.

WIDOW 1: That letter you from the mill—

MARLENE: I signed it.

WIDOW 1: I know you signed it.

MARLENE: All right then.

WIDOW 1: Was it for real, or are you going to change your mind and take the mill to court?

MARLENE: No.

WIDOW 1: Which one?

MARLENE: Which one what?

WIDOW 1: Which one no? Wasn't a yes or no question.

MARLENE: No, I'm not going to get into this.

WIDOW 1: You can't blame me for wondering why you turned that money down.

MARLENE: My reasons were mine. You got what you want.

WIDOW 1: No baby, the one thing I wanted was the one thing I can't have back again. And you can feel mighty as you want for refusing blood money. But some of us got kids. Thanks for the smoke.

(MARLENE and WIDOW 1 exit in opposite directions. Shift over to BO in the mill. CHAMP approaches him, reaches into his pocket and tosses him SUNNY's keys.)

CHAMP: Here you go.

Bo: Thank you. *(Takes keys)* You know I don't like to—
(Pause) Well, it's nothing you don't know about.

CHAMP: *(He changes into mill jacket and hardhat from his locker.)* No.

Bo: No big secret. *(Pause)* Did she fuss about the keys?

CHAMP: Not at all.

Bo: I figured she wasn't going anywhere, but I felt better knowing she couldn't.

CHAMP: I don't blame you.

JEMISON: *(Approaching)* All right. Quitting time.

CHAMP: What are you doing here still?

JEMISON: Waiting on your ass to get here.

CHAMP: Why is my ass so special?

JEMISON: Just because it is.

Bo: Jeff Smyer ain't coming in.

CHAMP: Bet his ass is grass.

Bo: He's got good reason. I'm going to have to put you down on the furnace though.

CHAMP: Aw, man.

Bo: Got to. I can't be short there tonight.

CHAMP: I fucking hate the furnace.

JEMISON: Got to keep them fired all night. Got to be fast.

CHAMP: I ain't feeling fast.

JEMISON: You ain't looking fast either.

CHAMP: Come on Bo. Send someone else. I ain't been on furnace in months.

Bo: Everybody's at it already. Don't want to shuffle people around now.

CHAMP: Hey, man, why am I late? Do me a favor. You owe me.

BO: I know, I know. I'll pay up some other night.

CHAMP: Shit.

JEMISON: Night always goes by fast on the furnace.

CHAMP: For you maybe.

JEMISON: And my night's fast gone. I'm taking off. Pray for a sunny morning.

BO: Then I won't sleep none.

JEMISON: Got to give a little to get a little.

BO: Yeah, why don't you get a little.

JEMISON: I'm on my way home to do just that.

CHAMP: Get some for me.

JEMISON: You look like you had more than you can handle, sweet son.

BO: Don't talk about my sister like that.

CHAMP: Get you home, Jemison.

JEMISON: I'm out of here.

CHAMP: 'Night.

JEMISON: *(Shakes hands with* BO*)* 'Night.

BO: 'Night.

*(*JEMISON *exits.)*

BO: Well, let's go. We got a lot of heats to fire tonight.

CHAMP: Who's taking my place on the caster?

BO: I am.

CHAMP: *You* are. Why don't you go on the furnace?

BO: My back's fucked up.

CHAMP: Aw, that's a load of shit.

BO: God's truth.

CHAMP: How did you fuck up your back?

BO: Old football injury.

CHAMP: Man, that's my excuse.

BO: It works for you.

CHAMP: That's because I really did play football.

BO: No, I'm really having some problems with it.

CHAMP: You are?

BO: Yeah.

CHAMP: Bad?

BO: Yeah. I'm taking these muscle relaxers. *(Pats his shirt pocket)*

CHAMP: Those will fuck you up good.

BO: I know. Not supposed to take them before work.

CHAMP: Give them to me. I'll take them for you.

BO: Too late now. Come on. Let's move. We got a lot of work tonight.

CHAMP: I'm moving.

BO: Not near fast enough.

CHAMP: Faster than you, old man.

(They exit. The WIDOWS appear down front.)

WIDOW 2: It's always that way, when something bad happens. People always say they felt it.

WIDOW 3: They felt something bad in the air.

WIDOW 1: Had a premonition. Were overly concerned.

WIDOW 2: More concerned than usual.

WIDOW 3: Had a funny feeling.

WIDOW 1: Said goodbye like they meant it.

WIDOW 3: See you in the morning.

Widow 2: Drive careful.

(Lights up on MARLENE *in the bed. The phone rings three or four times. She wakes, startled, and answers.)*

MARLENE: Hello.

(Lights flash up fast and bright, freeze-framing MARLENE *in the "hello". Lights fast out. Blackout.)*

END OF ACT ONE

ACT TWO

(The WIDOWS *escort* MARLENE *on stage, dressed in lab coats over their black dresses. One* WIDOW *takes the pack of cigarettes from* MARLENE's *pocket, hands one to her and returns the pack to* MARLENE's *pocket. Another* WIDOW *lights the cigarette for* MARLENE. MARLENE *accepts these ministrations, but does not acknowledge them. The* WIDOWS *exit.* JEMISON *enters into the area that will be the hospital, carrying two styrofoam cups of coffee.)*

JEMISON: Marlene. Hey. I brought you some coffee.

MARLENE: What.

JEMISON: I got a cup of coffee here for you.

*(*MARLENE *takes it.)*

JEMISON: That's a girl.

MARLENE: Yeah, I'm a good girl.

JEMISON: You doing real good.

MARLENE: Not for long if they don't fucking let me in there.

JEMISON: Doctor says that—

MARLENE: Bo's been in there.

JEMISON: Bo rode in the ambulance.

MARLENE: I don't see what—

JEMISON: His hands got burned.

MARLENE: Did they.

JEMISON: So I hear.

MARLENE: Where was his gloves?

JEMISON: I don't know.

MARLENE: Don't he wear gloves? Fireproof gloves.

JEMISON: Everybody does.

MARLENE: Fireproof suit. Safety glasses. Hardhat. Steel-toed boots.

JEMISON: Marlene.

MARLENE: To keep him safe.

JEMISON: Nothing going to do that.

MARLENE: Yeah?

JEMISON: Nothing going to keep you safe.

(Shift to the WIDOWS, *entering above. While they speak,* SUNNY *will enter, dressed in a robe and looking ragged.)*

WIDOW 2: It's usually a wrong number. That call that comes at two A M.

WIDOW 3: Make you jump out of your skin.

WIDOW 1: Count your children.

WIDOW 3: Count your blessings.

WIDOW 1: Count ten, breathe deep, pick it up. Cradle it against your cheek.

WIDOW 2: Cradle the receiver, rock it like a baby. Nice baby, good baby.

WIDOW 3: Don't cry. Don't cry.

SUNNY: Bo! Bo! You home Bo? Bo!. *(No answer)* Shit! *(She considers replacing the phone on the cradle, but lays it back down on the table and exits.)*

(Shift back to hospital. JEMISON *and* MARLENE *sit.* BO *approaches still in mill clothes, his hands bandaged in gauze.)*

MARLENE: Bo.

JEMISON: Hey Bo.

BO: Hey y'all.

MARLENE: Get me in there now Bo.

BO: In a minute.

MARLENE: Now.

BO: Jemison.

MARLENE: Bo!

Bo: You called Sunny?

JEMISON: Last I called it was still busy.

BO: Well call her again, and if she don't answer, go get her for me.

JEMISON: All right. *(Starts off)*

BO: Wait— *(Digs in his pocket)* Here's her keys. She can bring herself.

JEMISON: You sure you don't want me to bring her? I'm coming back anyway.

BO: Just give her the keys.

JEMISON: O K, I'll be back soon. *(Exits)*

BO: Marlene.

MARLENE: Enough of this bullshit Bo. Nobody's telling me nothing. I'm so scared. I never been so scared.

BO: They're going to let you see him now.

MARLENE: Oh god.

BO: And they wanted me to tell you—

MARLENE: Tell me.

BO: They wanted—

MARLENE: Shut up.

BO: Marlene—

MARLENE: Just shut up. Where is he.

BO: Room I just came out of.

(BO *takes* MARLENE *toward a door, but is met by the*
WIDOWS. *He exits as* WIDOW 1 *takes* MARLENE *downstage,*
while the other two WIDOWS *enter, flanking* CHAMP.
CHAMP *stands in front of the bed.* WIDOWS 2 *and* 3 *will cut*
a pair of mill pants and a T-shirt from him as they speak,
with the calm/efficient bustle of nurses.)

WIDOW 1: We just want you to be prepared.

WIDOW 3: So your expectations will be realistic.

WIDOW 2: We don't mean to scare you.

WIDOW 3: We don't mean to discourage you.

WIDOW 1: This is what we know about this sort of
thing.

WIDOW 2: When a patient is burned over eighty
percent of his body.

WIDOW 1: With burns of second and third degree.

WIDOW 2: There are factors in the recovery.

WIDOW 3: The skin is the largest organ of the body.

WIDOW 1: The rest of the body must work very hard to
compensate for the injury.

WIDOW 3: Obviously dehydration is a factor.

WIDOW 2: There is a great deal of danger from bacterial
infection.

WIDOW 3: A great deal of danger.

WIDOW 1: There is bacteria in the air we breath.

WIDOW 2: In the sterile bed.

WIDOW 3: In the human touch.

WIDOW 1: Wear this. *(Ties a surgical mask on* MARLENE*)*

WIDOW 2: He's heavily sedated now.

WIDOW 3: Heavily sedated.

WIDOW 2: We have him on painkillers.

WIDOW 1: Antibiotics. For any possible infection.

WIDOW 3: We don't mean to frighten you.

WIDOW 1: We only want you to be prepared.

(CHAMP *is now naked before her.* WIDOWS 2 *and* 3 *lie him on the bed, spreading his arms and legs apart.* WIDOW 1 *leads* MARLENE *to the bed. The* WIDOWS *stand away, apart from the action.)*

MARLENE: Champ. Champ. *(She removes the mask, reaches towards him, then pulls back.)* Champ.

CHAMP: Come to bed. It's time to go to bed.

MARLENE: Champ. *(She gingerly climbs onto the bed, and touches him at the hollow of the throat.)*

CHAMP: That's good. That feels so good.

(MARLENE *kisses the hollow of his throat.)*

WIDOW 1: What the hell are you doing?

(WIDOW 1 *yanks* MARLENE *from the bed and drags her downstage.* CHAMP *rises and exits as the other two* WIDOWS *strip the bed bare.* WIDOW 1 *and* MARLENE *struggle with one another downstage.)*

MARLENE: I'm just—

WIDOW 1: Do you realize—

MARLENE: I'm trying to tell you—

WIDOW 1: I think you ought to—

MARLENE: Let go of me!

WIDOW 1: Help me! Orderly! I need some help here!

MARLENE: Get off of me!

(BO *enters and grabs* MARLENE *from behind.)*

WIDOW 1: Calm down! I need some help here.

MARLENE: Get this bitch off of me! *(She manages to get a hand free and slaps* WIDOW 1 *across the face.)* Get off of me!

(They all leave the stage, and MARLENE *is alone, downstage center. She pauses, collects herself, reaches in her pocket and takes out a pack of cigarettes. She pats her pockets for matches. The* MINISTER *approaches her.)*

MINISTER: Church is filling up.

MARLENE: Is it.

MINISTER: It is.

MARLENE: You got a light?

MINISTER: I don't smoke. Sorry.

MARLENE: That's good you don't smoke.

MINISTER: I used to.

MARLENE: No vices now.

MINISTER: I got my bad habits.

MARLENE: No.

MINISTER: Yeah I do.

MARLENE: Like what.

MINISTER: This is a bad one.

MARLENE: I can't imagine.

MINISTER: At least I always feel bad about it.

MARLENE: How bad can it be?

MINISTER: I have a habit of eavesdropping.

MARLENE: Eavesdropping.

MINISTER: Yes.

MARLENE: Well, if that don't beat all.

MINISTER: Did she shake you up some?

MARLENE: Her? No.

MINISTER: You seem—

MARLENE: I am tired of being scrutinized.

MINISTER: I'm sorry if I—

MARLENE: Marlene, why you acting like this, Marlene, why'd you do that. I'm tired of everybody in my face.

MINISTER: Why'd you do it? Why did you sign your money away?

MARLENE: Jesus. *(Pause)* You want to know?

MINISTER: I'd like to know.

MARLENE: I don't want it.

MINISTER: That's it?

MARLENE: That's it. I just didn't want it. I didn't want them to feel better. To feel like they'd done their part. Give the sad little widow her sad little compensation. Pat her on the head. Send her off satisfied.

MINISTER: It was a good deal of money.

MARLENE: Not near enough. Not even close.

MINISTER: You wanted more.

MARLENE: You're not listening son. I did not want it. Not even a little bit. Because what is it really? What is that money they offer me? What is that?

MINISTER: It's your due.

MARLENE: It's bullshit. And every month of my life for the rest of my life there it would be in a brown envelope sitting in my mailbox. Every month of my life. You understand?

MINISTER: To a degree.

MARLENE: I got to go find me a light.

(MARLENE *and the* MINISTER *exit in opposite directions. She is met by* BO *and* WIDOW 1. *She collapses into their arms, as though sedated.* WIDOW 1 *helps* BO *get her into a*

chair, then he sits beside her, holding her. WIDOW 1 *exits.*
SUNNY *comes running on.)*

BO: Sunny.

SUNNY: You all right?

BO: I'm all right.

SUNNY: Jemison told me.

BO: Told you what?

SUNNY: Furnace exploded last night around two. Three
men already dead. Champ—

BO: Champ's dying.

SUNNY: He is?

BO: He will.

SUNNY: Oh no.

BO: Bad as he's burned he better hope he does.

SUNNY: How's Marlene?

BO: They knocked her out.

SUNNY: Why?

BO: She got hysterical. Tried to get in bed with Champ.
Hit a nurse.

SUNNY: She did?

BO: She did.

SUNNY: Where's Champ.

BO: Last room on the left. You going to go see him?

SUNNY: No.

BO: I think you should.

SUNNY: Will he know any different?

BO: I don't think so.

SUNNY: Then I don't think I will.

BO: Sunny—

SUNNY: What.

BO: I want you to.

SUNNY: Why?

BO: I just do..

SUNNY: Are you trying to—

BO: I'm not trying to do anything. I just want you to see him. I'm asking you to. Will you go see Champ?

SUNNY: *(Pause)* Yeah. I will.

BO: Thank you. *(Taking pill bottle from his shirt pocket)* Sunny, will you take the top off this pill bottle. I can't with these hands.

SUNNY: *(Takes pill bottle and looks at label)* They just give you these?

BO: No. Those are for my back. Doctor wanted to give me painkillers but I told him I was already taking these and he said they'd do.

SUNNY: You told him you were taking these?

BO: Yes.

SUNNY: Did you take one of these before work?

BO: I did.

SUNNY: You tell him that too?

BO: He didn't ask.

SUNNY: Well thank God for that.

BO: Sunny—

SUNNY: You know OSHA's going to be all over that mill. And here you are on the job taking fucking horse tranquilzers.

BO: Muscle relaxers.

SUNNY: They won't see any difference.

Bo: I was nowhere near that furnace when it blew.

Sunny: How'd you get burned, then?

Bo: Pulling them out of there after.

(Marlene *stirs.* Bo *quiets her.* Sunny *hands him the pills.)*

Bo: I need something to take those pills with.

Sunny: I'll get you some water.

Bo: Give me the bottle in your bag.

Sunny: Bo, I don't—

Bo: Sunny, you know it's in there and I know it's in there.

(Sunny *reaches in her bag and pulls out a pint of whiskey.)*

Bo: Take off the cap.

(Sunny *does, then hands* Bo *the bottle. He takes the pills, takes another shot. She reaches for the bottle to put the cap back on.)*

Bo: No, I'll just hang on to this for a while. Why don't you run on and see Champ now. Last room on the left.

Sunny: *(Hands him the bottle cap)* I heard you the first time. *(Exits)*

(The Widows *stand above, facing out, each holding a funeral urn full of ashes. As they speak they will scatter ashes on the ground in front of them.)*

Widow 2: For weeks it seemed it was sunny, bright.

Widow 1: Relentlessly cheerful.

Widow 3: I kept the venetian blinds cracked, and the air conditioner on.

Widow 1: And in the chill and the patterned light.

Widow 2: Watched the dust settle on the furniture.

Widow 3: And did not polish it once.

WIDOW 3: Toward September, when the tropical depressions develop on the gulf.

WIDOW 1: And hit the coast named as hurricanes.

(MARLENE *rises and joins them, going first to the bed, then coming downstage at the end of this section.*)

WIDOW 3: It stormed for three days straight.

WIDOW 1: Knocking the power out.

WIDOW 2: Scaring the kids.

WIDOW 3: I pulled up the blinds and threw open all the windows.

WIDOW 1: Let the rain blow through the house, clearing away the dust.

MARLENE: Clearing my head.

WIDOW 1: A slight scent of salt on the wind.

WIDOW 2: I put fresh sheets on the bed.

WIDOW 3: White sheets. Linen.

WIDOW 1: A wedding gift used only for company.

MARLENE: I stripped slowly. So slowly.

WIDOW 2: Rubbed oil into my skin. All over myself.

WIDOW 3: Spread the ashes on those clean white sheets.

WIDOW 2: And got into bed with my husband.

MARLENE: And when I was covered I wrapped myself in the sheets, went outside and let the downpour wash me clean.

WIDOW 3: In the backyard on the patio he built.

WIDOW 1: I let the rain wash me clean.

(MARLENE *drops to all fours, heaving.* BO *comes up to her and rubs her between the shoulders.*)

BO: Marlene, Marlene honey, you all right? Marlene.

MARLENE: *(Heaving)* I'm just sick.

BO: You want a nurse? I'll get you a nurse.

MARLENE: I'm just sick.

BO: You think it's what they gave you? Do you want some water?

(MARLENE waves BO away.)

BO: I'll get you some.

(BO starts off. The MINISTER and SUNNY approach.)

SUNNY: Bo, wait.

BO: I'm just getting—

SUNNY: Wait. *(She goes to MARLENE and holds her.)*

MINISTER: Mrs Hotchkiss, Mrs Hotchkiss. I'm sorry.

MARLENE: Oh, Jesus. *(Still heaving)* Oh Jesus. Goddamn.

SUNNY: *(Squatting down)* He passed quiet, Marlene.

MARLENE: You were there?

SUNNY: Yes.

MARLENE: You were with him when he died?

SUNNY: I was with him.

MARLENE: Goddamn it. Goddamn you all.

(MARLENE runs off, SUNNY follows.)

SUNNY: Marlene!

(BO exits. JEMISON enters and brings a chair downstage center. The MINISTER goes above and is helped on with a jacket as he passes the first WIDOW, handed a clipboard and glasses as he passes the next two. JEMISON should begin to speak as this is taking place. The MINISTER as the OSHA investigator should be different in tone and bearing.)

JEMISON: I gave Bo a call and he came in early. He was at the mill by nine-thirty and we discussed everything—which furnace was out, how high the creek was, how much dry scrap he had to work with.

MINISTER: And he understood all of this.

JEMISON: Every bit. There was plenty of dry scrap left.

MINISTER: Uh-huh. You said that the shift was shorthanded.

JEMISON: Yes sir.

MINISTER: And you had to stay until Mister Hotchkiss arrived.

JEMISON: Champ.

MINISTER: Yes.

JEMISON: Yes sir.

MINISTER: When he arrived did he seem to you to be impaired in any way?

JEMISON: Impaired?

MINISTER: Under the influence of alcohol or drugs?

JEMISON: No, he was not impaired, sir.

MINISTER: Now, you left before the actual explosion—is that right?

JEMISON: Well before it.

MINISTER: You left the mill at twelve-thirty, according to the guard at the plant gate, and the explosion was around two A M.

JEMISON: That's what I hear.

MINISTER: Yes. (Pause) Mister Jemison, in your opinion, what caused the explosion?

JEMISON: It could have been wet scrap. It could have been a gas tank in the scrap. It could have been a weak spot in the lining of the furnace wall. It could have been a lot of things. But I think it was just one of those things that happen. You know what I mean?

MINISTER: I'm afraid that I don't. Thank you Mister Jemison. *(He exits.)*

JEMISON: The pleasure was mine.

(JEMISON and the WIDOWS exit. BO enters, looking beat. SUNNY comes down the stairs and into the kitchen.)

SUNNY: How did it go?

BO: It went.

SUNNY: What did they ask you?

BO: Everything.

SUNNY: Like?

BO: Like what kind of scrap did we use to charge the heats, how high was the creek exactly, what time I got there, why Champ was late.

SUNNY: Did they ask about your medication?

BO: Company doctor told them.

SUNNY: And—

BO: I told them I was taking the medication as directed. Exactly.

SUNNY: They believe you?

BO: Why shouldn't they.

SUNNY: Because it's not true.

BO: I've told you already Sunny—I was nowhere near the furnace. The medication has no bearing.

SUNNY: That's the way you see it maybe, but these guys are trying to get the mill off the hook. These guys want to be able to pass it off on human error.

BO: Sunny—these guys want to find out what happened. Period. *(He puts the phone on the hook.)* Did you talk to Marlene today?

SUNNY: I tried.

BO: What did she say?

SUNNY: She said to tell the mill to shove their money.

BO: They want to settle.

SUNNY: Well apparently she doesn't.

BO: They told me that they want to settle out of court with everyone, and if any one of the women takes them to court, they'll settle with no one.

SUNNY: That's kind of them.

BO: It's just the way it's done I guess.

SUNNY: I think they're just trying to scare them.

BO: Well, I got to stay out of it. Let Marlene settle on her own. I can't get in the middle any more than I am already.

SUNNY: I don't think Marlene wants to settle at all. I think she meant just what she said.

BO: She's not thinking straight.

SUNNY: Thinking straight or not, she's made up her mind.

BO: I'll talk to her.

SUNNY: I don't think she'll talk to you.

BO: She'll talk to you.

SUNNY: I don't matter.

BO: Oh, man. *(Reaches to get pills from his jacket pocket)*

SUNNY: Does your back hurt?

BO: It's killing me.

SUNNY: Want me to rub it?

BO: No. I just need my pills. *(Looks at bottle)* I'm almost out of these.

SUNNY: You can't refill the prescription. You got to have the doctor write you another.

BO: Well, I'm not going to do that.

SUNNY: Why not? The OSHA thing is over.

BO: You know what they asked me?

SUNNY: What?

BO: They asked me to describe it all in detail. What I heard, what I saw. What I did.

SUNNY: Well of course they asked that.

BO: It was the way they asked it. Like they wished they'd been there to see it. To see the spectacular mill fire. Like when people ask me what the war was like.

SUNNY: What did you tell them?

BO: I told them it was like nothing they'd ever seen. Like nothing they'd ever want to see.

(BO *exits up the stairs,* SUNNY *watches him go, then exits. The* WIDOWS *enter with a set of sheets and pillows and make the bed as they speak.*)

WIDOW 1: After a time I stopped waking in the middle of the night.

WIDOW 3: Stopped feeling him lift the sheets and get into bed with me.

WIDOW 2: Stopped seeing him sitting at the kitchen table.

WIDOW 1: Drinking a beer, eating a sandwich.

WIDOW 2: While I had my morning coffee.

WIDOW 1: I can't say haw long it took for that to happen.

WIDOW 3: Because time was a funny thing then.

WIDOW 2: Maybe before Christmas.

WIDOW 1: Maybe at the start of the Little League season.

WIDOW 2: I just can't say.

WIDOW 3: But all of a sudden, he wasn't there anymore.

WIDOW 2: My life went on at my own rhythm.

WIDOW 3: Not from eight to four, from four to twelve.

WIDOW 1: From twelve to eight.

WIDOW 2: There was day and there was night.

WIDOW 3: And I started to sleep well, for the first time in my adult life.

WIDOW 1: Because the call had come.

WIDOW 2: And I was still in one piece.

(MARLENE *gets into bed, the radio blaring. She brings with her a mess of newspapers and mail.* BO *pounds on the door.*)

MARLENE: Come on in.

BO: (*Entering in mill clothes, he goes to the radio and switches it off.*) How you doing?

MARLENE: O K.

BO: I called over to your office but they said you were sick.

MARLENE: I guess I am.

BO: You need anything?

MARLENE: No. I just couldn't sit and look at a little green screen all day. I couldn't sit there all day.

BO: You called in sick all last week too.

MARLENE: You checking up on me?

BO: They volunteered that information.

MARLENE: They shouldn't have done that.

BO: Marlene—you're going to lose that job.

MARLENE: Am I?

BO: You keep up like this.

MARLENE: Like what.

BO: Girl, you know what I'm talking about.

MARLENE: Well Bo, if I lose the job I lose it. There are plenty of shitty jobs to be had in this world.

BO: May not be.

MARLENE: There always are.

BO: U S Steel laid off half their plant. More to come.

MARLENE: So?

BO: All those people with no money to spend. This town's going to look very different in a couple months.

MARLENE: They'll hire back.

BO: Not this time.

MARLENE: They're just trying to scare the union.

BO: Not this time.

MARLENE: Well, if there's not a shitty job to be had here, there's one somewhere else.

BO: You've never lived anywhere else.

MARLENE: Maybe it's time then.

BO: Marlene—people been asking about you.

MARLENE: People?

BO: Yeah.

MARLENE: And what do these people want to know?

BO: They want to know why you're holding up the settlement to the other women.

MARLENE: Why I'm holding it up.

BO: You each got a letter from the mill. A release.

MARLENE: Saying I won't take the mill to court.

BO: Yeah.

MARLENE: *(Holds up letter)* You mean this?

Bo: *(Takes it and looks at it)* How long you had this?

MARLENE: A while.

Bo: How long is that?

MARLENE: I don't know. A while.

Bo: Mill's not paying out until all of you sign this. I don't know what you're doing, but it ain't right.

MARLENE: Plenty of things ain't right with this world, Bo.

Bo: *(Looking at letter)* This letter says you turned down the money.

MARLENE: That's right.

Bo: You turned it down.

MARLENE: Turned it down and will not in the future take the mill to court.

Bo: You haven't signed it.

MARLENE: I will.

Bo: I don't believe this.

MARLENE: You want to see me do it?

Bo: No I don't. I want you to listen to me.

MARLENE: I know what you go to say.

Bo: Take the money.

MARLENE: I don't want it.

Bo: You stop this shit. Stop it. You call them mill. You tell them you're taking the settlement and you tell them you want a straight release, same as everyone else.

MARLENE: I told the mill that this was what I wanted.

Bo: And I'm telling you—

MARLENE: Don't you tell me what to do.

BO: You need to be told.

MARLENE: Don't.

BO: You might not want the money now—

MARLENE: I don't want it now.

BO: But a couple years down the line—

MARLENE: I won't want it then either..

BO: How can you know that?

MARLENE: I know it. *(Snatches pen from his pocket and signs the letter)*

BO: I don't believe you're doing this.

MARLENE: Believe it. *(Holds letter out to him)* Why don't you drop this off at the front office on your way into work?

BO: *(Crumples letter and throws it at her)* You take it to them yourself. *(Turns to head out, turns back)* You know Marlene, if you change your mind—

MARLENE: I won't—

BO: If you change your mind, a letter like that will never stand up in a court of law.

MARLENE: It won't have to.

(BO heads out.)

MARLENE: Hey Bo—

(BO turns back.)

MARLENE: How's your back?

(BO exits, MARLENE smooths the letter and puts it in an envelope. She exits. Shift over to JEMISON. Loud music is playing and he is drinking a beer. BO approaches him.)

JEMISON: Hey buddy.

BO: Hey.

JEMISON: You want one of these?

BO: No.

JEMISON: Sure?

BO: Just give me a hit of yours.

JEMISON: I'll get you one of your very own.

BO: No, no, no.

JEMISON: *(Hollers)* Hey! Janelle! Bring Bo here a Pabst.

BO: All right.

JEMISON: What time you got to be there?

BO: Sunny said around seven.

JEMISON: Plenty of time. *(Hollers)* Janelle! Cup of gumbo too! *(To* BO*)* You want one?

BO: No.

JEMISON: Just one! One gumbo, two beers! *(To* BO*)* So how you doing, man?

BO: Me? I'm fine.

JEMISON: How'd your shift run?

BO: It ran.

JEMISON: Yeah.

BO: You going?

JEMISON: Yeah I am. I'm not on until midnight.

BO: That's right.

JEMISON: Any of your shift coming?

BO: Most of it. Yours?

JEMISON: Some. Mill should have closed down for it.

BO: Never happen.

JEMISON: Just saying they should. Would have been decent.

BO: They're not in the business of being decent.

JEMISON: Come again?

BO: You heard me.

JEMISON: Man, never thought I'd hear you badmouth your employer.

BO: I'd hardly call that badmouth.

JEMISON: For you it is.

BO: Well maybe it is.

JEMISON: I'm not saying you—

BO: What you saying?

JEMISON: It's about damn time is all.

BO: Yeah.

JEMISON: They danced on your ass for quite some time.

BO: Don't I know it.

JEMISON: And Marlene—

BO: Marlene called her own shots.

JEMISON: It still sucks.

BO: Yeah, it does.

JEMISON: Just covering their own ass is all.

BO: They do it well.

JEMISON: Too well. This memorial service thing is the best part.

BO: What?

JEMISON: Memorial service. The mill put it together.

BO: Where'd you hear that?

JEMISON: Everybody knows.

BO: How come I don't.

JEMISON: I don't know. I mean what did you think Bo? Did you think First Baptist came up with this all by their selves?

BO: I don't—yeah. Yeah that's what I thought. Why not?

JEMISON: Why? Why should they do something like that. Do they need to look good?

BO: I guess not.

JEMISON: How much P R do the Baptists need in Alabama?

BO: I'm so fucking stupid.

JEMISON: No.

BO: I am.

JEMISON: No man, you just got other things on your mind.

(BO exits. JEMISON hollers out:)

JEMISON: Janelle—hey—I don't want no cold gumbo and warm beer!

(JEMISON exits. The WIDOWS enter.)

WIDOW 1: At first the checks came weekly. There it was every Friday.

WIDOW 2: Just like he was still on payroll.

WIDOW 3: Not as much as when he was on payroll. But just like.

WIDOW 1: Not as much. I'd get to Friday and there'd be nothing

WIDOW 3: There'd be food in the fridge for the next day or so. But nothing beyond that.

WIDOW 2: Then it was one of those holiday weekends. Lincoln or Washington or something. And the check didn't come.

WIDOW 1: Monday came and it still was not there.

WIDOW 3: Tuesday, Wednesday.

WIDOW 2: I borrowed from my sister.

WIDOW 3: And gave the mill a call.

WIDOW 1: Got passed from office to office. Forwarded down the line to pension and benefits.

WIDOW 2: The pension and benefits lady says all benefits are paid monthly.

WIDOW 3: Once a month, around the first.

WIDOW 1: It had come to her attention that checks were coming to me weekly.

WIDOW 2: And that was not the way things were done.

(The WIDOWS *exit. Shift to* BO *coming downstairs, half dressed and in pain.* SUNNY *waits for him in the kitchen.)*

SUNNY: I called the mill.

BO: What for?

SUNNY: You're not going in.

BO: Sunny—

SUNNY: Bo, where's your brains? You can't hardly walk.

BO: I can walk.

SUNNY: Yeah, and does it feel good? Does it feel fine? No, it doesn't.

BO: All right, all right.

SUNNY: I want to call the doctor too.

BO: Don't call the doctor.

SUNNY: Why not?

BO: I don't need to see him.

SUNNY: Why not?

BO: I'll be fine. I just strained it is all.

SUNNY: Strained it? You're having back spasms. You didn't fucking strain your back.

BO: No.

SUNNY: So can I call the doctor?

BO: Call your doctor.

SUNNY: My doctor?

BO: Yeah, your doctor.

SUNNY: I don't know if he can prescribe—

BO: Your doctor or no doctor at all.

SUNNY: Hey Bo, what's going on.

BO: Same shit that's been going on.

SUNNY: I thought OSHA was through.

BO: They finished with me a couple weeks ago. Then there was the mill management and the insurance company and even the fucking union had to jump in on it.

SUNNY: You're a foreman. You're not union.

BO: Champ and the other guys were.

SUNNY: I'm sorry.

BO: Yeah.

SUNNY: Why didn't you say anything?

BO: Say what?

SUNNY: Say they're putting you through hell. Tell me these things.

BO: Just out of practice, I guess.

SUNNY: Out of practice.

BO: You understand?

SUNNY: Yeah. I do.

(BO *and* SUNNY *exit together, she supporting him and rubbing his lower back. The* WIDOWS *enter above, holding their coffee cups.*)

WIDOW 3: I've heard that when a person's soul leaves his body, there's a moment.

WIDOW 2: A moment of decision.

WIDOW 3: The soul looks back on the body

(MARLENE *enters, smoking a cigarette, and stands downstage center.* CHAMP *enters from behind her, dressed again in the full reflective suit and hardhat, as at the top of the play.*)

WIDOW 3: Wracked with disease, age or injury

WIDOW 2: And decides either to return to the body

WIDOW 3: Or to pass beyond. Leave it behind.

(CHAMP *brushes a hand through* MARLENE's *hair, then stands aside, on the periphery.*)

WIDOW 1: I don't know if that's true.

WIDOW 2: If that really happens.

WIDOW 3: But I like to think so.

(SUNNY *approaches* MARLENE, *dressed as at the top of the play.*)

MARLENE: You've been scarce.

SUNNY: I've been down in the parish hall.

MARLENE: Doing what?

SUNNY: Watching churchwomen make coffee and finger sandwiches.

MARLENE: I'm not staying to make nice at some shitty little reception.

SUNNY: No one's asking you to.

MARLENE: Bo will.

SUNNY: No he won't.

MARLENE: Yes he will.

SUNNY: Marlene—what can you be thinking?

MARLENE: What do you mean?

SUNNY: What can you be thinking about Bo?

MARLENE: He's the best company man I know.

SUNNY: Girl, you got your head right up your own ass.

MARLENE: Do I Sunny? Do I really?

SUNNY: Without a doubt.

MARLENE: Well I think he's been looking pretty good through this whole thing.

SUNNY: Any reason why he shouldn't?

MARLENE: You tell me.

SUNNY: You know as well as I do.

MARLENE: You tell me.

SUNNY: I'll tell you what you already know because you seem to need to hear it. Bo had nothing to do with it. You know it, OSHA knows it, the company, the union, everybody knows it. So whatever you got going on in your head about Bo—you got to let it go. Because it's not about anything he did or did not do. It's you. That's all it is. It's just you.

(At some point during this speech, BO enters, unnoticed by either MARLENE or SUNNY, and stands back from them.)

MARLENE: He held me down.

SUNNY: What?

MARLENE: Held me down. Did not ask me what was going on. Did not try to find out. Held me down and let them sedate me.

SUNNY: You're talking about the hospital?

MARLENE: It was right here. *(Strokes the hollow of her throat)* Right here. I thought how strange that was. Right where his shirt collar would have been open his skin was untouched. Unburned. They let me into the room after they'd shot him full of morphine and left him to die.

BO: Marlene.

(BO approaches them.)

MARLENE: What Bo.

BO: No one left Champ to die. They did everything—

MARLENE: Yeah. They did everything. And then left him to die. I wanted him to die. Once I saw him I knew. He was so—raw looking. His eyes were way deep inside him. Nothing coming in or out. I talked to him but there was nothing coming in or out. So I touched him. Here, right here. *(Strokes the hollow of her throat)* The one place I could. Ran my fingers back and forth, light as air. His eyes came forward from back out of his head. Came to me. Locked in, focused. He said, clear as day he said, "Come to bed. It's time to go to bed." And I was so afraid. His arms and legs placed apart so they wouldn't touch each other. Spread across the bed. A small strip of space alongside him. I made myself as narrow as I could on that strip. Lay down next to him and felt the heat rise off his burned skin. Saw it. I ran my fingers along his throat. And he said, "That's good. That feels so good."

WIDOW 1: *(Calling down from where she stands above)* What the hell are you doing?

MARLENE: I'm just.

WIDOW 1: Do you realize—

MARLENE: I'm trying to tell—

WIDOW 1: I think you ought to.

MARLENE: Let go of me.

(SUNNY *approaches* MARLENE.)

WIDOW 1: Help me, orderly! I need some help here!

(SUNNY *reaches for* MARLENE.)

MARLENE: Get off of me!

WIDOW 1: Calm down! Come on! I need some help here!

(MARLENE *shrugs off* SUNNY, BO *grasps her and holds her:*)

MARLENE: Get this bitch off of me! Get off of me! Let me go! Let me go!

(MARLENE *is suddenly quiet.* CHAMP *turns and slowly walks off.*)

MARLENE: It wouldn't have made any difference to him. But to me. It would have been all the difference in the world.

(BO *and* MARLENE *stand for a moment,* BO *still holding her. Then they move apart.*)

BO: Marlene.

MARLENE: Yeah.

BO: Is there anything would make any difference now?

MARLENE: I don't know.

BO: I'd like things to be different with you and me. Or same as they was.

MARLENE: That's not going to happen.

BO: I want things to be better.

MARLENE: You do.

BO: I want it. You know I do.

MARLENE: Just like that. Because you want it.

BO: Don't you want that too?

MARLENE: Let's get out of here.

BO: You want to go?

MARLENE: I don't want to be here, do you?

BO: If you don't, I don't.

MARLENE: I never wanted to be here.

BO: Sunny?

SUNNY: Whatever.

BO: You don't mind?

SUNNY: Got no reason to.

BO: All right.

SUNNY: I'll get my car. It's out back.

MARLENE: I'm walking out the front.

SUNNY: Church is full of people.

MARLENE: That's even better. You going to come with me?

BO: Yeah, I'll come with you.

SUNNY: I'll bring my car around front.

BO: I got mine here.

SUNNY: Well.

BO: Come on, Sunny, what's your worry? People have always talked about you.

SUNNY: Bo!

BO: Well, you gave them something to talk about.

SUNNY: Somebody's got to. *(Pause)* O K. Let's go.

(Allowing MARLENE *and* SUNNY *ahead of him:)*

BO: You look good Marlene. That's a pretty dress.

MARLENE: Thanks. Sunny helped me pick it out.

(They all exit.)

WIDOW 3: So why are you here?

WIDOW 2: I'm here to heal. How about you?

(Fade, blackout)

END OF PLAY